This Book Belongs to:
_____

Plains Cree

This series is dedicated to my late mother, the matriarch of our family. You were the glue that held us together—our strength, love, and compassion. Your kindness and generosity touched everyone you met. Though you left us too soon, your spirit continues to guide and inspire us. We honor your memory every day, carrying forward the legacy of kindness and resilience you left us with. We love you and miss you dearly, Mother, Sister, Aunty, Friend, Wife, and Kohkom. This is for you. This is for you.

Theresa Wade Oct 3, 1959-Jan 26, 2021

Blue Thunder Woman loved spending time with her Kohkom Theresa.
Blue Thunder was captivated by Kohkom's stories about their Cree traditions.

One night as it grew darker, waves of green, blue, and purple flares of light danced across the skies.

"Kohkom! What's that in the sky?" She curiously asked Kohkom Theresa.

Kohkom was smiling as she glanced up at the starry sky, "Those are the Northern Lights, my girl. We refer to them as the 'Wawahtewa.' Ages ago, our people often told stories about them. Do you want to hear one?"

Blue Thunder gave an excited nod. Getting ready for the story, she cuddled up next to Kohkom Theresa.

"The Northern Lights are said to be the spirits of those who had gone ahead a long time ago, our ancestors and loved ones," Kohkom Theresa said. "Our loved ones were not just ordinary spirits; they are our ancestors from above and keep watch over us."

"Do they really watch over us?" asked Blue Thunder.

"The spirits dance across the skies to remind us that we are never alone. Even on the darkest days, they guide us; they are always with us."

"The Northern Lights are a symbol of our peace with the land and one another. The more peace, kindness, and love we have, the more the lights dance."

Blue Thunder looked up at the sky again. Like waves, the lights danced in smooth swirls and streaks across the sky, just as Kohkom had described.
"Kohkom, do you think I'll ever see the spirits dancing only for me?" Blue Thunder questioned.
Kohkom smiled kindly, "I believe you've already done that, Blue Thunder. They are always there waiting for us to watch them dance."

Kohkom and Blue Thunder looked up into the sky in silence for a long time. It looked as though the spirits of their ancestors were alive, dancing and watching over mother earth from the skies.

Every time the Northern Lights danced across the sky, Blue Thunder remembered the important lessons Kohkom had taught her.
She realized that the lights were more than just a beautiful sight; they were a gentle reminder of the love and protection that our ancestors have for us, always watching over and guiding us.

The legends of the Northern Lights have been passed down from generations to generations for our people to look up and see their loved ones dancing over the night sky. A peaceful reminder of the beauty of life. The End.

Cree Words:

Kisik: Sky
Wawahtewa: Northern Lights
Nimihito: Dancing
Nikamohk: Sing
Kohkom: Grandmother
Miyosiwin: Beautiful

My journey into writing these teachings began with the desire to educate my own children, which evolved into a mission to teach my children's dad as well—who had been in foster care from a young age till he aged out—about Indigenous culture. Through my books, you not only impart knowledge but also honor my late mother's memory, preserving and sharing the wisdom she generously provided during her lifetime.

Looking ahead, we are excited to expand the series to feature other First Nations languages so that youth from various Indigenous communities can connect with and learn their own languages. In addition to empowering the next generation, we also hope to educate the older generations who might be reluctant or apprehensive about pursuing knowledge and assist them in embracing their cultural identity through language and traditions.

Copyright © 2024 by Sue Ellen Wade

All rights reserved. This publication may not be reproduced, stored in a retrieval system, or transmitted in any form or by any means—electronic, mechanical, photocopy, recording, or otherwise—without the prior written permission of the author, except for brief quotations in reviews or critical articles. For permissions beyond these uses, please contact the author directly.

Designed and Created by: Sue Ellen Wade
Editor: Mya Wade
Published by: Sue Ellen Wade
Cree Translator: Leonard Rocky Wade
Email: sueellenwadedesigns@gmail.com
Website: creationssw.myshopify.com

www.ingramcontent.com/pod-product-compliance
Lightning Source LLC
Chambersburg PA
CBHW041442010526
44118CB00003B/150